PATRICE MARTY

Oracle of the

CRYSTAL
SKULLS

AF129955

REDFeather™
MIND | BODY | SPIRIT
4880 Lower Valley Road, Atglen, PA 19310

Thanks to all the guardians of the crystal skulls for being a part of this oracle. Thanks to ADMV and Françoise for their participation.

CONTENTS

INTRODUCTION

This oracle of 52 cards is based on the Mayan legend of Guatemala which, according to Shaman Grandmother Flordemayo, mentions 4 sets of 13 ancient skulls, not only 13 crystal skulls as many believe.

By soaking up the energy given by the skulls and perceiving the messages they convey to us, we are made to work with the energy of the heart. The draw is always fair, although it can surprise us and cause us to ask ourselves questions. The card that is chosen has its importance at the present moment on our own journey and allows us to receive the information gathered by the skull and to relate to its various connections.

We can connect with the skulls if we allow ourselves to open up and welcome meditation—this contact must not be made by the mind but by the energy of the heart chakra, located in the middle of the body. The heart chakra is between the three lower chakras, attached to the physical body, and the three upper chakras, attached to the spirit. The heart chakra is the point of balance between all the chakras; it is the connection with our being of light that allows us to be in harmony with ourselves and with others.

This is the work that the crystal skulls offer us, at our own pace, respecting our spiritual development. The goal is to be fully embodied on Earth and in harmony with all living things.

Our ability to open up and understand the skulls will improve and increase the more we use this oracle. In addition to the message transmitted by each skull, you will enjoy their stories and meeting their guardians.

Beyond the messages received and shared by their guardian, each skull has its own properties, which you can benefit from as you work with it.

You may not fully experience the message of the card at the time you pull it. It can last for several days or happen during your dreams.

You shouldn't expect anything except to be open to synchronicities, to new encounters, to your dreams, and to the messages of life.

Center yourself in the heart . . . welcome . . . and let yourself be guided by the crystal skulls!

The Sirius skull on the Pyramid of the Moon in
Teotihuacán, Mexico

Discovering the
CRYSTAL
SKULLS

The crystal skulls represent one of the greatest puzzles that archeology and modern science have encountered in recent decades.

The Legend

The Mayans have always been considered the "keepers of time" and "keepers of the skulls." One of their legends says that originally there were 12 inhabited planets in the universe, each of which gathered their knowledge in a crystal skull.

Long preserved in a pyramid called "the Arch," these skulls would have been given to men by the Itzas, the Atlantean people, to share their knowledge with human people. Atlantis has always been part of the oral tradition of Amerindian people, and the Atlanteans were said to receive their knowledge from Heavenly Initiators.

Over time, several civilizations, including the Olmecs, the Aztecs, and the Mayans, have been the guardians of these skulls and used them for their ceremonies.

But, when these civilizations abruptly vanished, it turned out that the rest of Western humanity was not ready to receive this knowledge. Also, during the Spanish conquest, the skulls were scattered throughout Central America by priests. It was imperative that they remain separate, their collective power being too powerful to be used wisely by humans.

The Mayan legend explains that the day when all these skulls, carrying major information on the history of humans and ancient civilizations, come together, they will deliver to humanity a message about its origin and future.

But the legend also warns that when that time comes, mankind must first be sufficiently developed and evolved, both morally and spiritually, in such a way that they will not abuse this great knowledge.

Ceremony in Palenque with the Lacandons tribe of Mexico.

Reality

Even today, the crystal skulls are a mystery as deep as the pyramids of Egypt, the Sphinx, the Nazca lines in Peru, Stonehenge in England, or the long skulls from all over the world.

Since their discovery—the first one happened between 1920 and 1924 during an archeological dig in Belize, Central America—crystal skulls have been the source of much controversy in the archeological and scientific world.

One thing is certain though. Explorer F. A. Mitchell-Hedges's skull from Belize, with its detachable lower jaw, is made of a very pure and rare rock crystal. A finding that is interesting, considering the tools now required to cut crystal, such as diamond grinding wheels or, more recently, the laser.

Today there are several ancient skulls whose discovery or acquisition is not really known. No one seems to be aware of their age, how they were made, what they were used for, or where they came from.

It should also be noted that several of these ancient skulls were brought to the British Museum in 1996 to be analyzed. The results from the crystal skulls Max and Sha Na Ra were withheld by British Museum experts, refusing to share their findings. So what did they find?

On the other hand it is worth mentioning that crystal is known in the scientific world for its use for information storage (in the RAM of computers). That's why the Mayan belief that crystal skulls are some sort of ancient "holographic computer" does not seem unfounded, even to modern science.

The so-called contemporary skulls can acquire, like the ancients, a certain amount of information, either through contact with ancient skulls, on sacred sites during travel, or in ceremonies.

This oracle is a great tool to share the energy conveyed by these crystal skulls and help as many people as possible to reconnect with this energy of love!

Chakras

The word *chakra* is derived from Sanskrit and means "wheel" or "disc." The term is better known today to designate "energy centers" that are located in the human body. According to this concept, there are seven main chakras and thousands of secondary chakras.

The seven main chakras are described as forming a luminous column that runs from the base of the spine to the base of the head. Each chakra is associated with a certain color, a duo of deities, a classic element, sounds, an organ of action, a sensory organ, and functions of consciousness. For example, the opening of the sahasrāra-chakra, the "thousand-petal chakra," corresponds to the unfolding of the kuṇḍalinī and is equivalent to spiritual awakening.

The oldest known mention of the chakras is found in the Upanishads, specifically the Brahma Upaniṣhad and the Yogatattva Upaniṣhad.

Number	Name	Sanskrit	Location	Color	Function
1	Root chakra	Muladhara	Located at the base of the spine, perineum	Red	Captures the energies of the earth to redistribute them in the body, especially in the feet, legs, sacrum, kidneys, and all the bone structure
2	Sacral chakra	Svadhisthana	Located three fingers below the navel, sacrum	Orange	It energizes the pelvis, lower back, sexual organs, and intestines. Determining our impulses and dependencies, testifying to our connection to our emotions and our pleasure, the sacral chakra corresponds to the relationship with the father, and to the acceptance of law and authority.
3	Navel chakra	Manipura	Located three fingers above the navel, in the pit of the stomach	Yellow	It interacts with the diaphragm, the digestive system (stomach, rat, faith ...) and the muscles. It is the seat of emotions, of undigested events, and of the relationship with the group, with others, and with social life.
4	Heart chakra	Anahata	Located in the hollow of the chest	Green and pink	It influences the circulatory and respiratory systems, the heart, of course, and the thorax but also the immune system and the first six backbones. The heart chakra allows self-love and relationships with others. Unique because central, it bridges the three lower chakras and the three upper chakras.
5	Throat chakra	Vishuddha	Located at the base of the throat	Blue	It intervenes on the throat but also the cervical vertebrae, the mouth, the arms, and the lungs.The throat chakra makes the connection between personal reality and the outside world and allows the expression of the individual.
6	Third-eye chakra	Ajna	Located between the two eyebrows	Indigo	It interacts with the face, eyes, nose, forehead, and spinal cord. The third eye allows you to look beyond appearances to know the essence of things. It opens awareness and intuition.
7	Crown chakra	Sahasrara	Located above the skull, at the level of the fontanel	Purple	It interacts with the brain and the central nervous system. The last chakra is the one that connects us to our inner self and to the universal consciousness.

SYMBOLS for Chakra Chart

How to use this
ORACLE

This is not an oracle like the others . . .

Before using it for the first time, take a moment to center yourself at heart level and welcome it. Take the necessary time to feel as though you are in touch with this oracle. Handle it, lay out each of these cards, contemplate them, feel them without any demand or expectation. This greeting time will create a sacred space between this oracle and you, which will benefit you during your various draws.

These skulls are waiting to be welcomed and called upon to enter into action. Gratitude will help you welcome their interventions with more depth, so don't forget to thank the skull(s) at the end of the draw.

Different Readings/Draws Available

Before each draw, make yourself comfortable in a serene location, place your intention at the heart chakra level, and connect to your being of light. Spread out the oracle cards and make room for your intuition before drawing a card with the left hand, the hand of the heart.

"Meditation Card" Spread

- Depending on your needs or your desires, you can draw a card to meditate or to set an intention.
- Concentrate on the image of the skull and its name, learn about its history, and listen to the message he has sent to you.
- Now let yourself be filled with the energies of this skull and its connections, either by putting your hand on it or just with your gaze, depending on how you feel. One method that is effective is to place the card (photo of the skull facing up) in front of the heart chakra.

- And now let go of what should be released and welcome what is coming, for as long as you need.
- Messages and answers can be expressed in different ways, either through feelings, visualizations, images, dreams, or your inner "little voice." Then give thanks for the message.

Two-or Three-Card Spread

- Center yourself and put your intention at heart level. Draw the first card while thinking about a specific subject, a project, or a problem.
- Depending on your intuition, you can make a new draw now or in a few days. A second skull will be complementary, a support to the first.
- Regularly make a connection with the skulls and your initial request. Keep the cards drawn together until the blockages are unlocked or the project is successful, which often takes place in stages.
- Depending on the progress of your request, you have the possibility of a second card. This third draw could bring a new idea or thought, a different and additional energy.
- Throughout this period, listen to messages, record your dreams, and look for synchronicities.

"A Guide for the Night" Spread

- To be done just before going to bed.
- Use the same method as the one-card draw / read it, then slip the card under your pillow or place it vertically facing you on the bedside table.
- This approach gives you the possibility during your sleep to be guided by this skull on different "travels" (astral, akashic, galactic). It will also have an impact on the way you dream.
- In the morning, remember to thank the skull!

"52-Week" Spread

To live a deeper spiritual journey with the energy of the 52 skulls, you can make a weekly draw for 52 weeks, so a different crystal skull will accompany you each week for a full year!

This layout is not to be taken lightly; it is a commitment to spiritual evolution, and hard work is required . . . it will become a part of your life. It will bring you clarity and help you be more in line with your life's mission: to walk a path to becoming a being of light.

- Begin on the Sunday of each week (in connection with the sun).
- Make yourself comfortable and center yourself at the heart chakra level.
- Connect with the oracle.
- Shuffle the deck three times with your intention of spiritual evolution.
- Take the card that presents itself, skull faceup, and discover your skull of the week.
- Place the rest of the cards near you. The oracle is complete and participates in its "Unity."
- Place the card in front of you or on your heart chakra and take a moment with this card so that it helps you release what is not working for you and welcome what is right and appropriate for you at this moment.
- Make sure you are grateful, since that will help open your heart chakra and the connection with your being of light.
- Have no expectations and no judgment of what you can see or feel, and continue this meditation every day with the skull for the week.
- Keep this skull close to you throughout the week in order to maintain the link and stay aware of your request.
- Do not hesitate to ask for help if you feel any discomfort.

Note: The drawn cards must be put aside in order to benefit from the energy of the 52 skulls.

The Mayans considered the number 52 sacred because it was the number of years in a "bundle," a unit similar in concept to our century. They used two calendars (the Tzolkin, divinatory cycle, and the Haab, for agricultural use). The sacred 52-year cycle called the "Calendar Cycle" combines these two calendars.

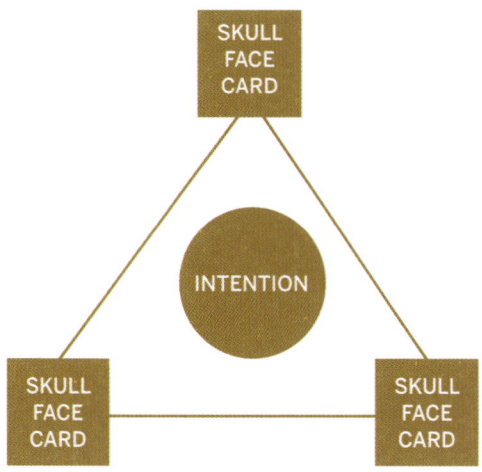

Sacred Geometry Spread

- Make yourself comfortable and center yourself at heart level.
- Draw a circle on a piece of paper. Write down in the center of the circle an intention, a specific subject, a wish, a project, or a problem, but be sure to word it in a positive way. For example, instead of writing "To no longer be sad," say, "To be happy."
- Take the necessary time to visualize and feel your request written in the circle.
- Then shuffle the cards 3 times by connecting to the oracle in its full Unity and pick 3 cards as they come to you. Place these 3 cards around the circle, in the shape of a triangle, with the summit pointing upward and the skulls on each card facing up (see Fig. 1).
- Place the first card at the base of the triangle on the bottom left, place the second card on the bottom right, then place the third card at the top of this triangle.
- Place the remaining pile of cards, skulls facing down, at the top right of the triangle. The oracle is fully present with you.

- Be grateful for these sacred powers, whether they are skulls or geometric shapes. This will make it easier to open your heart chakra and connect with yourself.
- The energy of these three skulls will bring help and reinforce the intention so that your request may be realized.
- Let this sacred geometry (the circle, the triangle, and the square), this trinity, these waves of shapes come into action!
- Place this "mandala" in a place where you will see it frequently during the day for seven days, or for 14 or 21 days if you want to intensify your request. It is even recommended that you meditate once a day with this mandala. Your ability to follow these steps, your motivation, and your involvement have a considerable impact in its realization.
- If your initial request was unsuccessful, perhaps it has changed; so do not hesitate to rephrase it. The resolution of a blockage or the success of an intention often occurs in different stages.

The circle where you place your intention: This is a symbol of spirituality, femininity, life—everything comes from the circle! It is also a protection. It represents the union, the energy, and the circulation of the energy, which is concentrated in its center.

The triangle formed by the three cards: This is a symbol of stability, hierarchy, success, and spiritual elevation. It is both union and harmony, but also power and divinity. It is akin to the Trinity, to the triad. It points up, so that the base of the triangle lays the foundation, while the stability then rises to other heights. This forms a pyramid-like arrow, rising to the sky, evoking success!

The square shape of the cards: This represents the symbol of materiality, masculinity, stability, discipline, rigor, respect, and perfection. It also evokes the four cardinal points or the four alchemical elements (fire, air, water, and earth). The square relates to the materialization, the achievement, the happening of the idea according to Plato.

The Therapeutic Spreads

"Bath of Light" Spread

This "Bath of Light" will allow you to reharmonize and strengthen your different bodies.

Its oval shape is linked to that which radiates around the Virgin of Guadalupe in Mexico. (**See figure 2**. The tilma, or "apron," of Juan Diego, on which the Miraculous Virgin appeared in 1531, even today still draws much devotion and raises questions with all its mysteries.)

We could also call this Bath of Light the "Bath of Liberation and Protection."

- Focus on the heart chakra level and connect with the oracle.
- Shuffle the cards three times, placing your intention on your "Bath of Light" request.
- Take the cards in the order they have been shuffled, skull facing you, and place them one at a time, creating an oval shape in which you will be able to lie down. Place each skull card side by side, facing the sky, with the jaw facing toward the center of your oval.
- If you have any cards left, keep them to your right, inside the oval, facedown. You can fully connect and engage with the oracle as a whole.
- Make yourself comfortable lying down in this sacred shape (use a pillow or yoga mat if needed), arms relaxed at your sides, in order to open yourself safely to welcome this "Bath of Light."
- Feel gratitude, which will make it easier to open your heart and feel welcome.
- When you are finished, thank each skull as you gather them.
- One session for 10 minutes every week is recommended.

Sponge Spread

In ancient traditions, asceticism is the art of listening. We listen with our whole body. And, of course, some bodies are more sensitive than others. The therapists of Alexandria, of Jewish tradition, living in the first century CE and who greatly influenced the Christian tradition, had a practice that closely resembles a Tibetan practice, and perhaps also a Sufi practice: it is that of the sponge!

You need to welcome everything coming from you, without fear, including pain and ugliness. But rather than keeping it all, you "squeeze" it out like a sponge.

- I breathe in: I welcome.
- I breathe out: I squeeze the sponge.

The skulls around you will absorb everything and transmute it into Light. Once cleansed and released, you can welcome the light again without keeping it, though. Learn to breathe out, to give peace without adding pain to suffering or emotion to your feelings.

- Focus on your heart chakra and connect with the oracle.
- Shuffle the cards three times, focusing on your intention. Then take the deck in your hands, with the skulls facing you, and uncover the cards one by one in the order of the deck.
- Take the necessary number of skull cards to create a circle in which you can sit in the center and place them, face up and facing the center of the circle, toward you.

- Make yourself comfortable seated in the center of the circle (*zafu*).
- Place the remaining skull card pile face down inside the circle with you.
- Concentrate on your breathing.
- You will notice that a vortex will gradually form around you to nourish and nurture you.
- Thank the skulls before gathering the oracle.
- This is recommended for 10 minutes, once a week.

"Inner Luminous Mast" Spread

The Inner Luminous Mast is the energy mast forward of our spine. It takes support from our physical center of gravity, the *Tan Tien* (gate of the universe in Chinese, 3 finger widths below the navel, in the thickness of our small pelvis, according to Chinese tradition). It ends at the top of our head.

This layout takes place on the ground, lying down. Cards form a line on the middle of the body, skulls facing up, jaws toward your feet, in the same orientation as your body.

- Focus on the heart chakra and connect with the oracle.
- Shuffle the cards three times, focusing on your intention.
- Choose the cards with the skulls facing up, and place them in the order they appear.
- In a seated position, legs stretched and open, place four cards, forming a line from your ankles to your pelvic floor—one card at the bottom of the calves, one on the top of the calves, one at the bottom of the femur, and one above.
- Once the four cards are placed between your legs, lie down with the oracle in your hands. Place one card facing up on your navel, and two cards on your chest (one between the breasts and one at the level of the heart chakra). Place the remaining oracle cards facedown on the ground on your right. You are then fully connected with the oracle.
- Stay in this position for 10 minutes and you will feel fully connected with yourself, free from emptiness, wounds, desires, and needs. You will reach Completeness.
- Teach yourself not to be distracted by your mind, which will try to lead you to restrictive or even negative thoughts.

- You will feel fully connected with everything as the energy of the skulls strengthens because they are connecting to your Inner World.
- You will enjoy realignment, peace, and serenity.
- Thank each skull as you gather the oracle.
- Recommended duration is 10 minutes, every two days maximum.

"Resources" Spread

"Let the necessary resources for your future come to you."

- Position yourself facing east. Place the cards on the floor or on a table, facing up in a triangular shape pointing toward you for a 15-minute sitting meditation.
- Focus on your heart chakra and connect to the energy of the oracle.
- Shuffle the cards three times and think of a precise question about your future or simply welcome your new resources without any requests.
- Choose the cards in the order of the deck, skulls facing you, and place them in a triangular shape pointing toward you:
    - First row: one card facing you, jaw down and facing the sky, which will be the point of the triangle.
    - Second row: above row 1, from left to right, two cards facing down
    - Third row: above row 2, always from left to right, three cards facing up
    - Fourth row: above row 3, place four cards facing down from left to right, which will be the base of the triangle.
- The skulls, whose faces are turned toward the ground, are unknown and active collaborators.
- Place the remaining oracle cards to the right of the triangle's summit, facing the ground. The oracle is fully engaging with you.
- Make yourself comfortable in front of your skull layout.
- Feel grateful, since it will help you open up your heart chakra.
- During these 15-minute meditation sessions, place your full attention on the heart chakra and your breathing so that your mind does not wander or interfere.
- Listen to the messages of the skulls as they accompany you on your journey.
- Let the resources offered come to you without judging yourself or the situation, and without expectations.
- Thank the skulls while gathering the oracle.

"The Clock" Spread

This spread will help you develop your knowledge, know-how, and how to be.

- With 12 cards, form the face of a clock with you at the center.
- Focus on your heart chakra and connect to the energy of the oracle.
- Shuffle the cards three times, setting your intention to develop your knowledge, know-how, and how to be.
- Take the cards from the top of your deck, skulls facing up, and place them in order of arrival as follows:
- Position the first four skulls in the shape of the four directions, skulls facing the sky, jaws toward the center. Place them in the following order: first skull in the North at twelve o'clock, second skull in the East at three o'clock, third skull in the South at six o'clock, and fourthth skull in the West at nine o'clock.
- Then take the following eight cards and place them with skulls facedown in the following order to complete the shape of a clock: start with one o'clock, two o'clock, four o'clock, five o'clock, seven o'clock, eight o'clock, ten o'clock and eleven o'clock. These skulls will be unknown collaborators.
- Place the remaining oracle cards on the outside, at three o'clock and facing down. The oracle is fully connected. Your clock is made!
- Make yourself comfortable, in a sitting position in the center, facing north.
- Place your intention at heart level and honor the Spirit of the Old Skulls.
- Thank them for welcoming you, for helping you to evolve in your way of being, of thinking, of receiving, of acting, all on the path of wisdom.
- Be careful that your mind does not interfere during your three minutes of meditation, which will then be renewed in the other three directions.
- Then position yourself facing the East, the rising sun, and start your meditation again.
- Then three minutes facing south.
- And end with your three minutes facing west.

Thank the Spirit of the Ancient Skulls and then each skull by gathering the oracle.

Subsequently, if the three minutes of meditation are easy for you, then you can go to five minutes, then seven, then nine per direction … at your convenience. An excellent practice for you!

The Card
MESSAGES

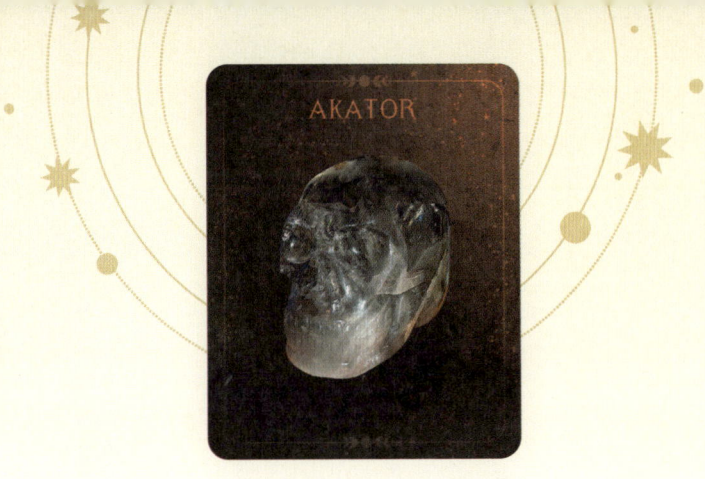

Sculpted in 2002, in Brazil

Material: Smoky quartz
Chakra: 1

Promotes rooting and refocusing. Calms emotions and improves lucidity and concentration. Helps you think better and get rid of anxieties and irrational fears. Improves self-confidence and the ability to open up to others.

Weight: 317 lbs. / 144 kg

This stone was found in a river following a dream I had. The skull was sculpted three years later.

"Akator came to teach about life and relationships."

His guardian: Leandro de Souza
Website: https://templeofalchemy.boutique/

Discovered in 1987

Material: Red/orange rutilated quartz
Chakras: 1 and 2

This stone accelerates healing and regeneration. Powerful ally for mental and spiritual well-being. Essential for good meditation. Stone of protection for astral travel, promotes communication with angels.

Weight: 1 lb. / 500 g

This skull was found in Mayan ruins. It was in a display case, stamped "artifact" in a store in Cuernavaca, Mexico. Alden vibrates with strong energy; it is a tool of divination in the psychic work of its guardian.

"If you pay too much attention to the gift wrapping,
you won't see the gift I'm bringing. My shape and size allow you to see me,
but my gift is to connect to higher frequencies."

His guardian: Jane Doherty
Website: www.janedoherty.com

Discovered in 2002, in the Himalayas

Material: Rock crystal or quartz
Chakras: All 7 chakras

Universal healing stone for receiving, emitting, and amplifying. Unlocks blocked energies, transmits energy to the body, realigns subtle bodies.

A stone that allows the awakening of consciousness, it helps develop concentration, intuition, telepathy, visualization, clairvoyance, and wisdom.

Weight: 6 lbs. / 2.70 kg

He is one of a group of 13 crystal skulls called "the Himalayan Crystal Skulls." Arriving in the United States in 2002, they were first presented to the public by Star Johnsen-Moser. In 2006, she became the guardian of Amakua and joined Xamuku to anchor the Light and the mystical archetypal multidimensional pattern of the Sacred Tree of Life.

"I am the heart of the Earth. I hold the old energies of our ancestors, our sacred roots, and help others connect and embody their true power of unconditional love."

His guardian: Star Johnsen-Moser
Website: www.starjohnsenmoser.com

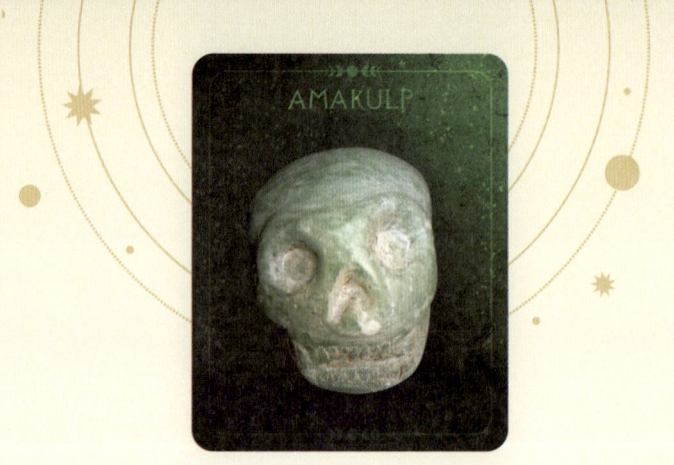

Discovered in 1950

Material: Green alabaster
Chakras: 4 and 7

Promotes the release of negative energies. Opens the heart chakra. Helps in soul-searching and the ability to forgive. Powerful stone to attract positive energy. Strengthens the ability to cleanse and purify the soul.

Weight: 11 lbs. / 4.9 kg

Discovered in the 1950s, near the site of the ancient Mayan temple of Palenque, in southern Mexico, on the edge of the Yucatán Peninsula, a few kilometers from Campeche Bay. His name was given to me in a dream the day before he arrived! (I don't know what that means.) Feminine energy; it works primarily on the upper chakras.

"I open and amplify the channel between the divine source and your sacred temple. I facilitate the expansion of your divine essence in love and joy."

His guardian: Patrice Marty
Website: www.moncranedecristal.fr

Discovered in 2006

Material: Rock crystal or quartz
Chakras: All 7 chakras

Universal healing stone for receiving, emitting, and amplifying. Unlocks blocked energies, transmits energy to the body, realigns subtle bodies.

A stone that allows the awakening of consciousness, it helps develop concentration, intuition, telepathy, visualization, clairvoyance, and wisdom.

Weight: 22 lbs. / 10 kg

It comes from a monastery in Lhasa, Tibet, where it had been used by Buddhist monks since the 1800s for healing and divination.

"It is essential to take the time for inner peace in order to make room to receive, create, and manifest. You have to stop, land, breathe, and receive. Be in peace, go in peace, live in peace. Peace in this world begins with peace within each individual."

Her guardian: Grace
Website: www.crystalskulls.com

Carved in the 15th century (Buddhist tradition)

Material: Ancient Himalayan rock crystal/quartz
Chakras: All 7 chakras

Universal healing stone for receiving, emitting, and amplifying. Unlocks blocked energies and realigns subtle bodies. Allows the awakening of consciousness.

The Dorje: Refers to the indestructible nature of the mind itself and of Awakening. It is a mark of power and royalty.

Gold
Chakra 7: Illuminates the mind and promotes connection with our being of light

Ruby
Chakras 1 and 4: Carrier of the vital energy of fire.
Connect to Earth. Divinatory stone.

Emerald
Chakra 4: Stone of absolute harmony and truth

Weight: 11 lbs. / 4.82 kg

This skull was transmitted to me by friends, "bearers of skulls," via an antique dealer in Tibet, on December 31, 2016. "Taken out" from a temple in Nepal, where it was kept by a single monk throughout his life. He was the only being allowed to touch it for ceremonies and care (probably, because it is very fragile with all its stones). It is decorated with a golden crown of fire with the most- intricate designs. Over 100 small rubies and 100 authentic emeralds decorate it! At the top of the crown is a quartz dorje to concentrate divine energy and wisdom.

"Immerse yourself in my gaze and connect with the energy
of the Himalayas resonating with high and pure spiritual energy.
The mountains are so high that cosmic energy is embedded in the
crystal and generates a karmic healing vibration to
increase your frequency."

His guardian: Patrice Marty
Website: www.moncranedecristal.fr

Carved between 900 and 1520 BCE

Material: Silver obsidian
Chakras: 1, 3, and 7

Black, gray, silver, with glitter; allows access to purity and humility. Protection stone (less powerful than black obsidian); promotes intuition and meditation. Facilitates the balance of our internal forces; stone of ying and yang.

Weight: 2.6 lbs. / 1.2 kg

When I acquired this skull, it was on deposit in a sales office in Bonita, California, deposited by a private collector. It comes from the Valley of Mexico and was certainly carved during the Aztec Postclassic period. It represents Mictlāntēcuhtli, god of death and lord of Mictlan (hell). A statue with similar eyes, cheeks, and teeth is preserved by the British Museum, which confirms the authenticity of this artifact. Many similar skulls can also be seen on a tzompantli, at the Templo Mayor in Tenochtitlán.

"Once in Mictlan, your superfluous wealth will be of no use to you."

His guardian: Alexis Bousiges
Website: https://aztecskull.blogspot.com

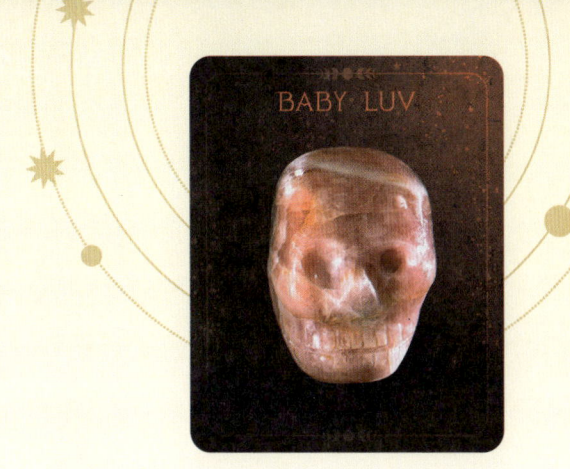

BABY LUV

Discovered in 1900

Material: Rose quartz
Chakra: 4

Stone of peace and unconditional love. Purifies and opens the heart, releases negative emotions, increases discernment and self-love. Strengthens empathy and the ability to love.

Weight: 17.6 lbs. / 8 kg

This skull was found in a burial mound near Luov, Ukraine, by an old Russian monk. It dates back to the Scythian Age (700 BCE). The skull was placed next to a row of gold works of art made by the Scythians. It was preserved by monks before it became the possession of a Russian family. They themselves were convinced that the skull, although it was used by the Scythians, actually belonged to the Cimmerians.

"Place me on your heart; let my message reach you."

His guardian: Joky Van Dieten

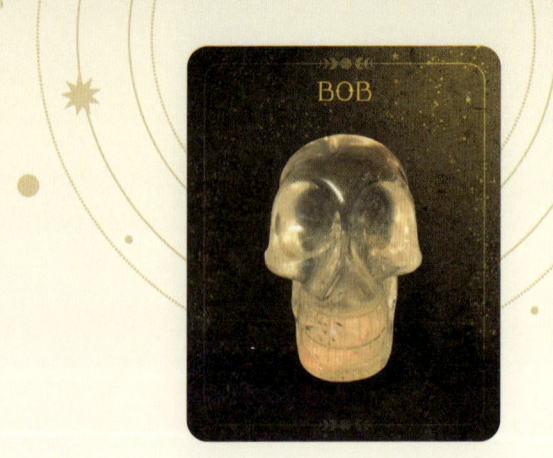

BOB

Discovered in 1990

Material: Rock crystal or quartz
Chakras: All 7 chakras

Universal healing stone for receiving, emitting, and amplifying. Unlocks blocked energies, transmits energy to the body, realigns subtle bodies.

A stone that allows the awakening of consciousness, it helps develop concentration, intuition, telepathy, visualization, clairvoyance, and wisdom.

Weight: 5 lbs. / 2.26 kg

This is the wish skull, found in Tucson in 1999. During a crystal festival, I heard it call me. He was sitting there on the window, waiting for me. Bob was activated at the September 9, 2009, and October 10, 2010, conference in Tempe, Arizona. He sat alongside the Mitchell-Hedges skull, Synergy, as well as the former AMI skull.

"Ask and it will be given to you. Seek and you will find. Knock and you will be heard. State your wish and it will be granted."

His guardian: Cece Stevens
Website: www.internationalastrologers.com

Discovered in 1897

Material: Rock crystal or quartz
Chakras: All 4 chakras

Universal healing stone for receiving, emitting, and amplifying. Unlocks blocked energies, transmits energy to the body, realigns subtle bodies.

A stone that allows the awakening of consciousness, it helps develop concentration, intuition, telepathy, visualization, clairvoyance, and wisdom.

Weight: 12 lbs. / 5.45 kg

This skull is probably European, dating from the 19th century. It was acquired through Mr. G. F. Kunz at Tiffany & Co., New York.

"Let us honor the wisdom of the ancestors; it guides
our steps toward a new world. Those who have walked the earth before us
know the way to go. Let us invoke them without delay."

Its guardian: British Museum
Website: www.britishmuseum.org

CANA IXIM

Discovered in 2008

Material: Blue jade
Chakra: 5

Symbol of purity. Brings calm and wisdom. Blue jade promotes compassion and creativity. Facilitates the development of confidence, patience, respect, courage, and responsibility.

Weight: 4 lbs. / 1.70 kg

Cana Ixim (pronounced *"Canna Ishim"*) means "the Lady of Corn." For the Mayans, corn is sacred because it represents life. This skull was used in Guatemala in ceremonies for healing, fertility, and abundance of crops.

"Give yourself permission to embrace the experience of infinite abundance for yourself. The more abundantly you receive, the more abundantly you can give and share with others. Spread seeds of joy and prosperity so that they can grow abundantly."

Her guardian: Grace
Website: www.crystalskulls.com

Discovered in 2002

Material: Rock crystal or quartz
Chakras: All 7 chakras

Universal healing stone for receiving, emitting, and amplifying. Unlocks blocked energies, transmits energy to the body, realigns subtle bodies.

A stone that allows the awakening of consciousness, it helps develop concentration, intuition, telepathy, visualization, clairvoyance, and wisdom.

Weight: 4.5 lbs. / 2 kg

Robert Rhodes bought a very unusual skull from a monastery in Nepal. When he acquired it, he knew that Clouds, due to its marks, was a very special skull and that it should travel. Robert had heard of Joky Van Dieten and her journeys around the world with her crystal skulls and contacted her. After a few letters, Clouds joined Joky and her crystal skull family. He traveled from Nepal to America then to the Netherlands, and now all over the world, giving everyone the chance to meditate in his company.

"Place me on your heart; let my message reach you."

His guardian: Joky Van Dieten

Sculpted in 1926

Material: Obsidian
Chakras: 1 and 3

It is the stone of protection! Acts against blockages, traumas, and fears. It opens up to spirituality. Facilitates communication with the parallel world. And it is the link between divine spirit and matter.

Weight: 8 lbs. / 3.5 kg

This is the only modern skull in Joky's collection, nicknamed "Darth Vader." It was carved from obsidian in Idar-Oberstein, Germany, in 1926. It is very popular with children, who love it because of its *Star Wars* look. One day, when it was arriving at the airport, a custom's officer hit the skull with a hammer on the jaw, believing it to contain drugs. Fortunately, only a small piece broke.

"Place me on your heart; let my message reach you."

His guardian: Joky Van Dieten

Date of discovery unknown

Material: Golden calcite
Chakras: 1, 3, 6, and 7

Reduces limiting beliefs. Contributes to courage and self-esteem. Promotes the radiance of our being. Facilitates memory of past lives and therapeutic visualization. Excellent for meditation.

Weight: 11 lbs. / 5 kg

Discovered in Mongolia, and full of feminine energy, she spent time with other ancient skulls. This type of skull always has the same round shape, with slight differences—large eye sockets, a very pronounced third eye, and missing teeth—which allow each skull to have its own vibrations.

"I act on the consciousness of the heart along with the Divine Mother: Mary, Shakti, Isis, the Saptamâtrikâ. . . . I am the mediator between the human personality and the divine nature. I facilitate clarity of mind and liberation of the mind."

Her guardian: Patrice Marty
Website: www.moncranedecristal.fr

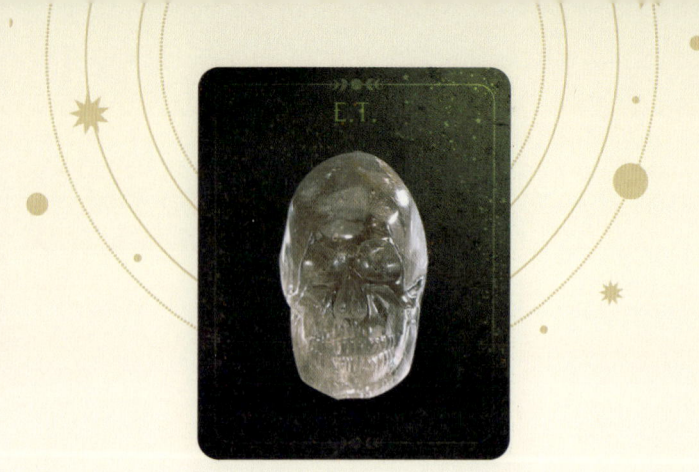

Discovered in 1906

Material: Smoky quartz
Chakra: 1

Promotes rooting and refocusing. Calms emotions and improves lucidity and concentration. Helps to think better and to get rid of anxieties and irrational fears. Improves self-confidence and the ability to open up to others.

Weight: 10 lbs. / 4.5 kg

The skull was discovered by a Mayan family while digging in their backyard in Guatemala. At a "Crystal Healing" symposium in Sedona, Arizona, in May 1999, E.T. was recognized as the lost skull of the Mayans. According to them, he came from the Pleiades. Mayan priests confirmed in a ritual that Joky was the right guardian and that she still had a long way to go. Joky acquired this skull in 1991.

"Place me on your heart; let my message reach you."

His guardian: Joky Van Dieten

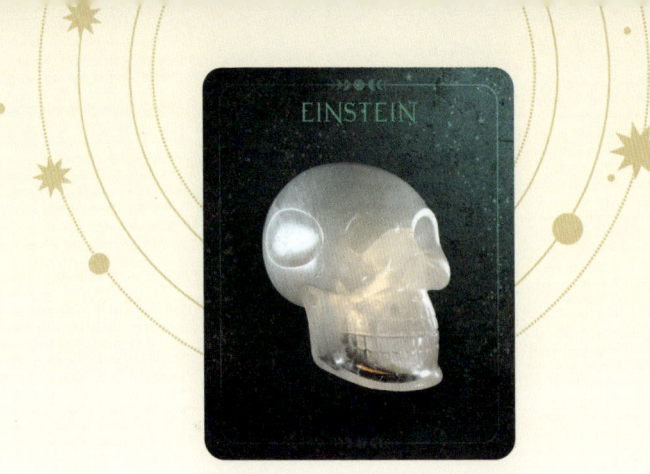

EINSTEIN

Discovered in 1930

Material: Rock crystal or quartz
Chakras: All 7 chakras

Universal healing stone for receiving, emitting, and amplifying. Unlocks blocked energies, transmits energy to the body, realigns subtle bodies.

A stone that allows the awakening of consciousness, it helps develop concentration, intuition, telepathy, visualization, clairvoyance, and wisdom.

Weight: 33 lbs. / 15 kg

It was discovered in Central America. It was first kept in a private collection of artifacts, then brought to Jack Frasl at a crystal store in Kirkland, Washington. Carolyn had asked Jack to find her a small skull. To her surprise, it was this skull he had acquired for her. When she met Einstein, she knew it was his skull.

"Skull of consciousness, I communicate in the language of light where everything is harmonious. Unconditional love is my signature. My goal is to raise the consciousness of humanity and awaken it to its true nature."

His guardian: Carolyn Ford
Website: https://einsteinthecrystalskull.com

Sculpted in 2016 in Cusco, Peru

Material: Rock crystal or quartz
Chakras: All 7 chakras

Universal healing stone for receiving, emitting, and amplifying. Unlocks blocked energies, transmits energy to the body, realigns subtle bodies.

A stone that allows the awakening of consciousness, it helps develop concentration, intuition, telepathy, visualization, clairvoyance, and wisdom.

Weight: 11 lbs. / 5 kg

This skull "came to me" during my trip to Peru in April 2016, during which I stayed a few days in Cusco. One morning, a person was in front of my hotel and offered me this skull. Quite coincidentally, this trip had the theme of elongated skulls, and I have been lecturing on this theme since 2015!

"I am the female energy of the ancients who populated this planet
and to which you can reconnect."

His guardian: Patrice Marty
Website: www.moncranedecristal.fr

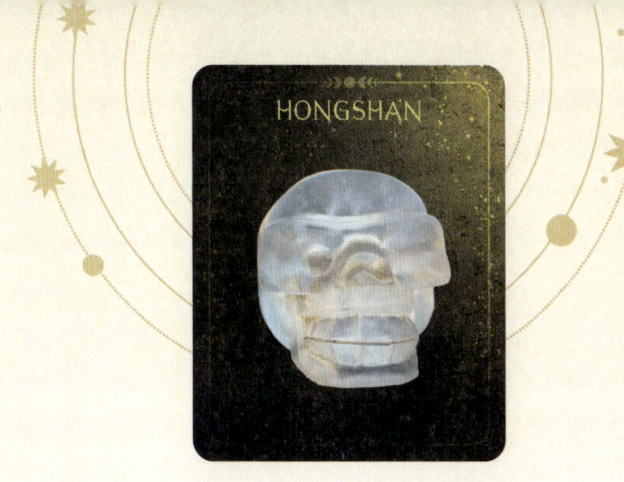

Carved during the Hongshan period (4700–2900 BCE), Inner Mongolia

Material: Vitrified sand
Chakras: All 7 chakras

Fusion of the sand obtained during a meteorite impact. Symbolizes cosmic energy and the connection between the earth and the universe. Stone of protection, it realigns our bodies and our chakras. Reharmonizes the electromagnetic field of the body. Represents strength, love, and balance.

Weight: 15 lbs. / 6.9 kg

With the same name as this Neolithic era, Hongshan joined Imanna and the Crystal Team in 2013. This skull is connected to the minds of the Mongol shamans he worked with. It is extremely powerful, and its mission is to cleanse, reharmonize, and realign people and places. Called the "Cleaner," he brings Light where there is shadow, he removes negative energies, he neutralizes difficult karmas, and he reharmonizes.

"Let go of what is not harmonious and find your original light."

Her guardian: Imanna
Website: www.imanna-crystalteam.com

Date of discovery unknown

Material: Brown jasper
Chakras: 1 and 2

Protection and determination, comfort and stability. Brown jasper helps us dissolve our physical and psychic blockages. Repairs the aura. Facilitates deep meditation.

Weight: 9 lbs. / 4 kg

According to some channelings, she would have spent time in Ephesus, where she was in contact with Mary Magdalene and Cleopatra. Houmama would have come to France with Marie-Madeleine and the Templars. It is impossible to date it, but erosion due to water, sand, and wind, as well as the stalactite concretions visible on the outside and inside of the skull, bear witness to its age. She participated in ceremonies on the sacred Feminine. It represents the matrix.

"Imbue each of your cells with the divine energy of the sacred Feminine of the Mother Goddess. Radiate your creative force of Love."

Her guardian: Patrice Marty
Website: www.moncranedecristal.fr

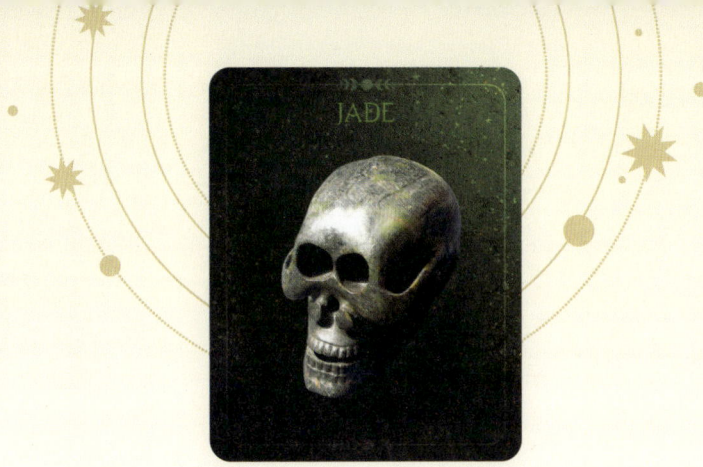

Date of discovery unknown

Material: Nephrite jade
Chakras: 4 and 6

Stone of protection against maliciousness and negative influences. Recommended for undecided people. Symbolizes honesty and temperance. Soothes the desire for possession. Increases the level of consciousness.

Weight: 10 lbs. / 4.5 kg

It was found in a tomb/temple in Mongolia along with other jade skulls and skeletons. These skulls have a seal impressedo n their tops. Some have an ancient script glyph on the back, which could be the spiritual name of Genghis Khan. It is possible that these items were collected from his tomb/temple.

"I have a heritage of interacting with humanity and providing possibilities for healing. I work with the energy of the heart. You who wish to receive healing from the Male and Female Divinity, call me and I will answer."

Her guardian: Kathleen Murray

Discovered before 1876

Material: Smoky quartz
Chakra: 1

Promotes rooting and refocusing. Calms emotions and improves lucidity and concentration. Helps to think better and to get rid of anxieties and irrational fears. Improves self-confidence and the ability to open up to others.

Weight: 8 lbs. / 3.5 kg

The first known king of Illyria was Hyllus ("the Star"), who died in the year 1225 BCE. The Illyrians kept his skull in a container of water and took it to battle and wherever they went. The container was allegedly struck by lightning. Fallen to the ground, the water, parts of the skull, and surrounding plants would have immediately crystallized in the form of this skull.

"Place me on your heart; let my message reach you."

His guardian: Joky Van Dieten

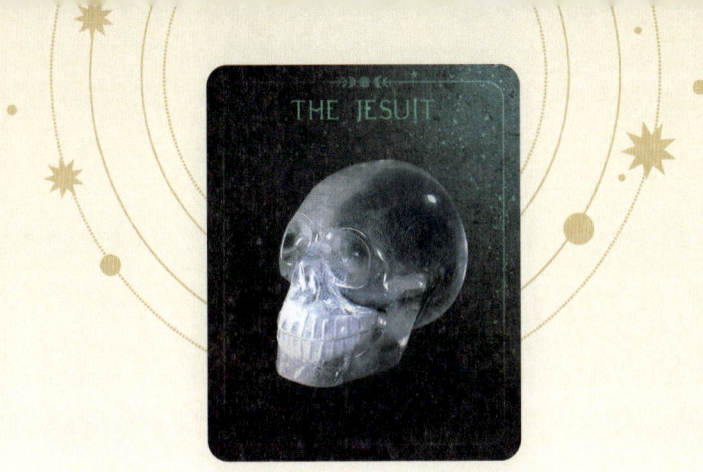

THE JESUIT

Discovered in 1534

Material: Rock crystal or quartz
Chakra: all

Universal healing stone, receiving, emitting and amplifying. Unlocks blocked energies, transmits energy to the body, realigns subtle bodies. Stone that allows the awakening of consciousness, it helps develop concentration, intuition, telepathy, visualization, clairvoyance or hearing, and wisdom.

Weight: 5.5 lbs. / 2.5 kg.

Its history dates back to the year 1534. It is believed that it may have some connection with Saint Francis of Assisi, who is well known for his love of animals. This skull came into Joky's possession in August 1993 and was given to him by the abbot of an American monastery, who was in dire need of the money.

"Place me on your heart; let my message reach you."

His guardian: Joky Van Dieten

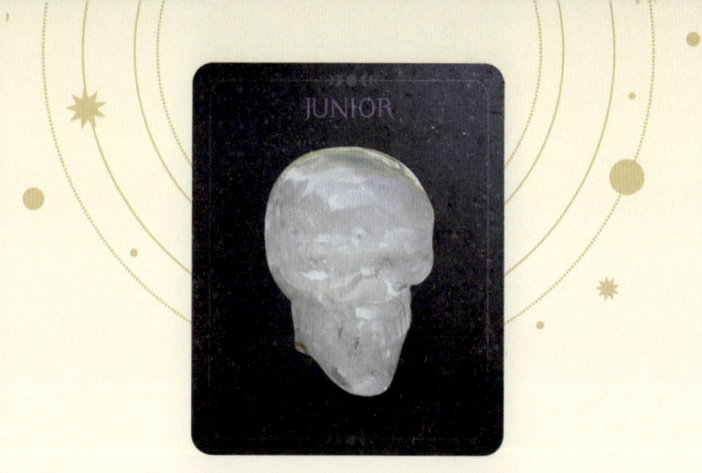

Sculpted in 1970 in Brazil

Material: Rock crystal or quartz
Chakras: All 7 chakras

Universal healing stone for receiving, emitting, and amplifying. Unlocks blocked energies, transmits energy to the body, realigns subtle bodies.

A stone that allows the awakening of consciousness, it helps develop concentration, intuition, telepathy, visualization, clairvoyance or hearing, and wisdom.

Weight: 10 lbs. / 4.53 kg

We have had Junior since 1997. He has participated in many ceremonies, drumming sessions, meditations, and various other events each year.

"The skull is the image of pure consciousness, of wisdom stripped of all attachments, hatred, and ignorance. The crystal symbolizes light and clarity. A symbol of wisdom, skulls help broaden our perspective, to see the interdependence of all things to increase our compassion for all sentient beings."

His guardians: Walter Hodgdon and Nels Gullerud

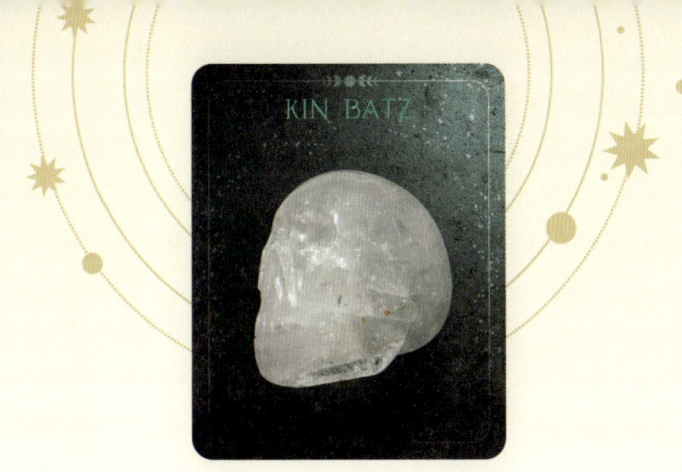

Date of discovery unknown

Material: Rock crystal or quartz
Chakras: All 7 chakras

Universal healing stone for receiving, emitting, and amplifying. Unlocks blocked energies, transmits energy to the body, realigns subtle bodies.

A stone that allows the awakening of consciousness, it helps develop concentration, intuition, telepathy, visualization, clairvoyance, and wisdom.

Weight: 17 lbs. / 7.70 kg

In 2000, Chan K'in Viejo, the last great Lacandón shaman of Mexico, passed the skull on to his grandson Kayum Garcia. The ceremony took place in Yakchilan, where prophecies were revealed.

"Allows a reactivation of the heart to the rhythm of unison, of the universe, in tune with Eternal Love. As the gatekeeper of the sacred Tzolkin calendar, he allows you to synchronize with the time of creation, to open your consciousness to the wisdom of the Ancients."

His guardian: Kayum Garcia, my Lacandón "brother"

LANZON

Dated 900 to 1300 BCE, from Chavín de Huántar, Peru

Material: Rock crystal or quartz from Peru
Chakras: All 7 chakras

Universal healing stone for receiving, emitting, and amplifying. Unlocks blocked energies, transmits energy to the body, realigns subtle bodies.
A stone that allows the awakening of consciousness, it helps develop concentration, intuition, telepathy, visualization, clairvoyance, and wisdom.

Weight: 5.9 lbs. / 2.70 kg

I received this skull after traveling to Chavín de Huántar. On this site, deep in Peru, we performed a ceremony underground, in tunnels where there is a huge monolithic statue of El Lanzón. There, I received the message to place a crystal at the foot of this statue; two months later, this ancient skull chose me as its guardian! It has many shamanic engravings, including snakes, a puma, and a spiral.

"I am the axis of the cosmos, the mediator between heaven and earth, the mediator of opposites; that is, I embody the principle of balance and order. Feel Lanzón's supernatural strength."

His guardian: Patrice Marty
Website: www.moncranedecristal.fr

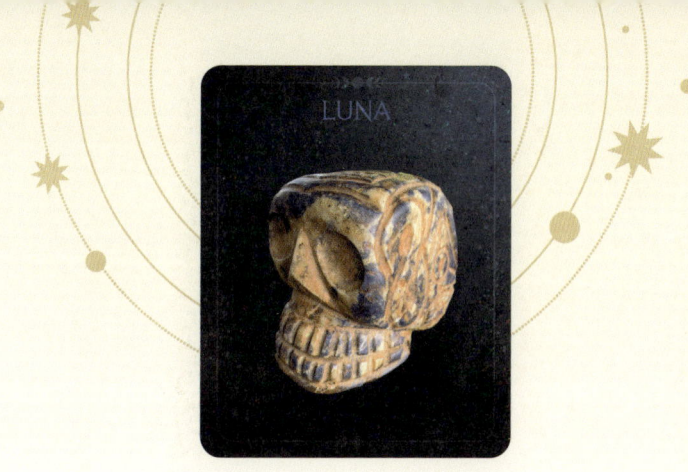

Date of discovery unknown, in Tiahuanaco, Bolivia

Material: Largely consists of lapis lazuli
Chakras: 5 and 6

Symbolizes sacred strength. Brings fullness and inner peace. A stone of communication and intuition. Helps develop honesty, compassion, and righteousness.

Weight: 7 lbs. / 3.3 kg

The Tiwanaku civilization, or Tiahuanaco, is a pre-Inca civilization that dominated the southern half of the central Andes between the 5th and 11th centuries. Luna is a "ball" of Love, feminine energy, who works to rebalance feminine and masculine energies (with Lanzón). She has shamanic engravings on her: the hummingbird, the puma, and serpents. Her nose is shaped like a pyramid.

"Let my animal totems accompany you on the path of love
for yourself and others, on your part, both feminine and masculine,
in order to spread limitless love in your turn."

Her guardian: Patrice Marty
Website: www.moncranedecristal.fr

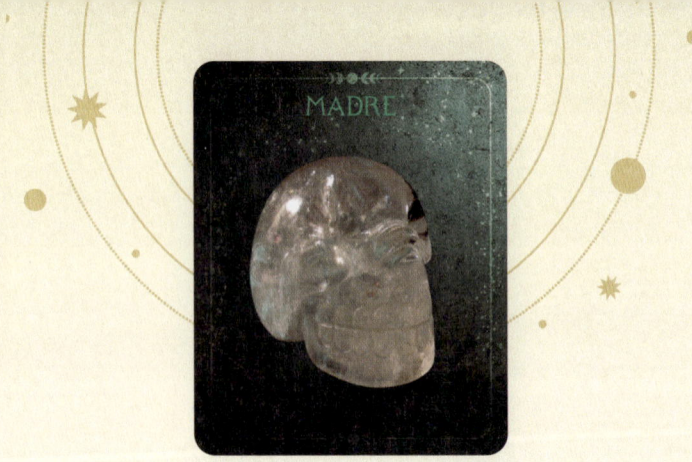

Discovered in 1998

Material: Rock crystal or quartz
Chakras: All 7 chakras

Universal healing stone for receiving, emitting, and amplifying. Unlocks blocked energies, transmits energy to the body, realigns subtle bodies.

A stone that allows the awakening of consciousness, it helps develop concentration, intuition, telepathy, visualization, clairvoyance, and wisdom.

Weight: 13 lbs. / 5.8 kg

Madre was purchased from a private collector. The skull says it came from the Orion nebula. Madre is the mother of the 13 Dolphin Skulls clan. They all have the nose of a dolphin. They honor the time when humanity was threatened with extinction and had to transform into dolphins and whales in order to live in the safety of the ocean.

"I am here to help women and men during times of transition in their lives, using the art and power of love. Meditate with me to discover true self-love. I am linked with the dolphins and can orient them toward you through meditation."

Her guardian: Laurie Walker
Website: https://crystalawareness.com

MAGNIFICENT FIRE

Date of discovery unknown.

Material: Red Jasper
Chakra: 1

Stone of anchoring and success. Helps regulate excessive energies. Allows you to refocus. Supports various addiction problems or obsessive-compulsive disorders. Provides help to stop difficulties in a more serene way.

Weight: 6.5 lbs. / 3 kg

This skull was found in Colombia in a cave near the Ecuadorian border at the Citadel Saphadana, near Rio d´Oro. The tribe speaks the Aramaic language.

"Place me on your heart; let my message reach you."

His guardian: Joky Van Dieten

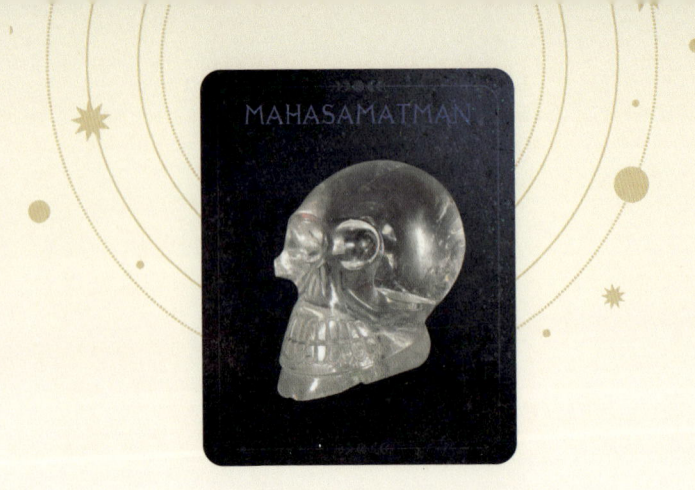

Discovered in 1996

Material: Rock crystal or quartz
Chakras: All 7 chakras

Universal healing stone for receiving, emitting, and amplifying. Unlocks blocked energies, transmits energy to the body, realigns subtle bodies.

A stone that allows the awakening of consciousness, it helps develop concentration, intuition, telepathy, visualization, clairvoyance, and wisdom.

Weight: 3.3 lbs. / 1.50 kg

The story of this skull is its manifestation in light through our ancestors in Orion. Appearing through a galactic portal known to native Brazilians, it holds the Orion archives that bring us star healing and help us unite with ourselves and our star ancestors.

"I am here to help understand the mission of the skulls.
We are one with you; we are you. I illuminate your journey;
I expand your consciousness and unite you with your stellar
brothers and sisters in Love and Peace."

Her guardian: Kathleen Murray

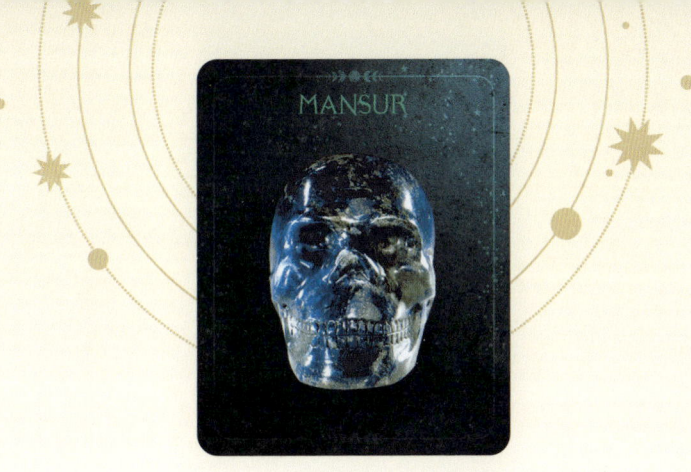

Discovered in 1995

Material: Lapis lazuli
Chakras: 5 and 6

Symbolizes the sacred force. Brings fullness and inner peace. A stone of communication and intuition. Helps develop honesty, compassion, and righteousness.

Weight: 4.5 lbs. / 2 kg

This skull was discovered in the Amazon rainforest by an Inca tribe from northern Peru. Tuki, the tribe's spiritual leader, recounted how they placed the skull in a cave to clean it before handing it over. They were convinced that the skull would benefit them more if they gave it to Joky.

"Place me on your heart; let my message reach you."

His guardian: Joky Van Dieten

Discovered between 1924 and 1926

Material: Rock crystal or quartz
Chakras: All 7 chakras

Universal healing stone for receiving, emitting, and amplifying. Unlocks blocked energies, transmits energy to the body, realigns subtle bodies.

A stone that allows the awakening of consciousness, it helps develop concentration, intuition, telepathy, visualization, clairvoyance, and wisdom.

Weight: 18 lbs. / 8.17 kg

Estimated to be several thousand years old, Max was discovered in Guatemala and used by Mayan priests for healing, rituals, and prayers. Then he was entrusted to Lama Norbu Chen, who opened a healing center in Texas. JoAnn and Carl Parks met him when their 12-year-old daughter, Diana, was dying of cancer. Before his death, the lama gave the skull to the Parkses.

Message for Peace:

For the mistakes that kill Earth/Mother

Efforts required for its rebirth

Love of humanity

Courage to rectify mistakes

Together we will recreate a better world.

Her guardian: JoAnn Parks

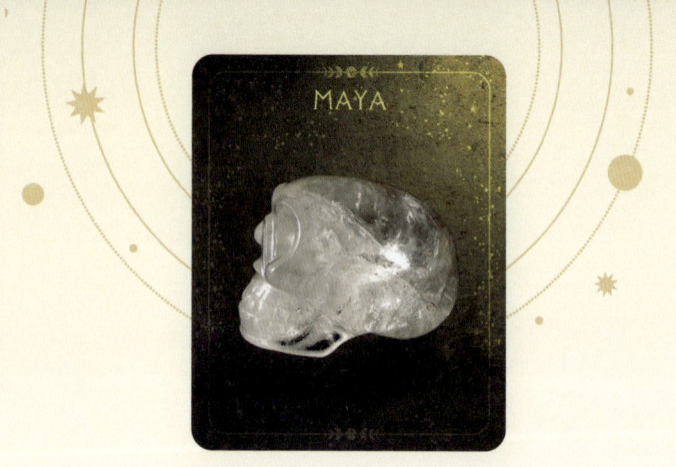

Discovered in 1987

Material: Rock crystal or quartz
Chakras: All 7 chakras

Universal healing stone for receiving, emitting, and amplifying. Unlocks blocked energies, transmits energy to the body, realigns subtle bodies.

A stone that allows the awakening of consciousness, it helps develop concentration, intuition, telepathy, visualization, clairvoyance, and wisdom.

Weight: 5 lbs. / 2.26 kg

Found in undetermined Mayan ruins (possibly Tikal). She was locked in a display case stamped "artefacts" in a store in Cuernavaca, Mexico. Maya has a gentle energy of transformation. She can take you to other dimensions. She has three rows of teeth and was the only Mayan crystal skull present at the solar ceremony at Chichen Itza on March 21, 1995.

"Remember to awaken your own inner light as you scan the crystalline layers. See all your facets and know that Love is God and God is Love."

Her guardian: Jane Doherty
Website: www.janedoherty.com

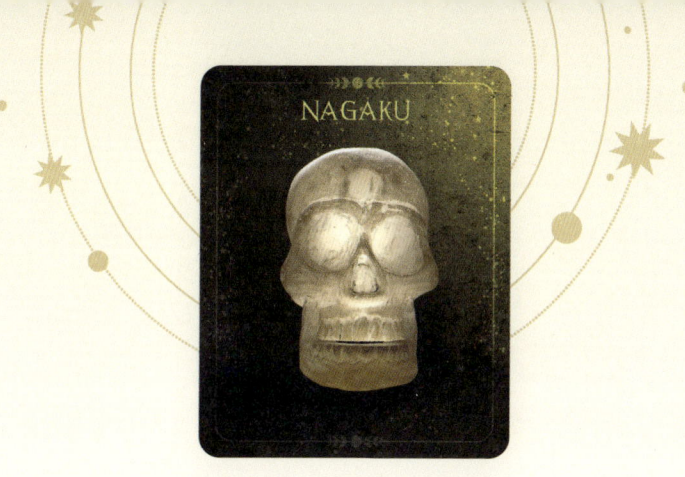

Discovered in 1938

Material: Rock crystal or quartz
Chakras: All 7 chakras

Universal healing stone for receiving, emitting, and amplifying. Unlocks blocked energies, transmits energy to the body, realigns subtle bodies.
A stone that allows the awakening of consciousness, it helps develop concentration, intuition, telepathy, visualization, clairvoyance, and wisdom.

Weight: 4.3 lbs. / 1.97 kg

It is one of 13 ancient crystal skulls found in caves in the Himalayas, near Tibet where the Dropa tribe lives. It was offered to Hunbatz Men, of the Mayan people, by its discoverer Dr. Frank Loo.
The main quality of this skull is clairvoyance.

"May the Great Spirit be with you always."

His guardian: Patricia Cardona
Website: https://cosmicmysteries.com

Discovered in Tibet (15th-century Buddhist tradition)

Material: Rock crystal
Chakras: All 7 chakras

Universal healing, receiving, emitting, and amplifying stone. Unlocks
blocked energies and realigns subtle bodies.
Allows the awakening of consciousness.

Red Coral
Chakra 7: Combines the beneficial forces of the three kingdoms—mineral,
plant, and animal—and concentrates all the cosmic energies in it.

Ruby
Chakras 1 and 4: Carrier of a vital energy of fire. Connect to earth.
Divinatory stone.

Emerald
Chakra 4: Stone of absolute harmony and truth
Fossilized yak bone: Considered by ancient Tibetan traditions as a
spiritual representation of the living in its different stages. With silver,
coral, and turquoise inlays.

Weight: 17.6 lbs. / 8 kg

Namaskar was used in a monastery in Tibet as a medium of deities and
oracles. Tenzin Wangyal Rinpoche blessed him and confirmed to Imanna
to continue the work of transmitting the messages of the subtle, Spirit worlds.
He lights the way by revealing what is on the other side of the veil, where
past, present and future are one.

"Enter into my gaze, open your third eye, and find the path
to knowing the worlds again."

His guardian: Imanna
Website: www.imanna-crystalteam.com

NEFERTITI

Discovered in 1997

Material: Chevron amethyst
Chakras: 6 and 7

Stone of peace and serenity. Purifies the aura. Soothes excesses, impulses, and addictions.

A true spiritual guide, she is recommended when learning meditation. Stimulates the third eye and facilitates clairvoyance and intuition.

Weight: 3 lbs. / 1.4 kg

Purchased from a private collector by DaEl Walker, director of the Institute of Crystal Consciousness. Upon examination, it had several unusual characteristics. Made of amethyst and hollow, it had a dolphin nose carved on its face, making it a member of the dolphin skull family. He is elongated, similar to the skulls of Pharaoh Akhenaton, his wife Nefertiti, and their children.

"I bring you the skills of ancient Egypt. Meditate with me and step into the higher levels of consciousness where time comes together, where past, present, and future are one."

His guardian: DaEl Walker
Website: https://crystalawareness.com

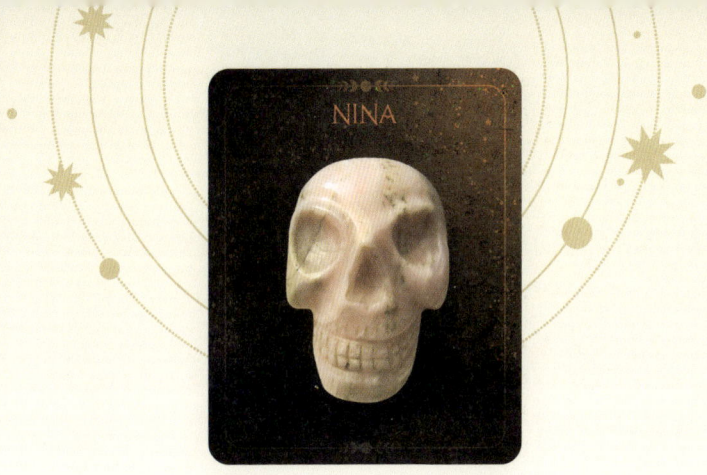

Date of discovery unknown

Material: Alabaster, manganese
Chakras: 4 and 7

Promotes fullness; very active in case of stress. Allows access to our awareness of being. Helps in introspection and the ability to forgive. Stone connected with our spirituality center.

Weight: 11 lbs. / 5 kg

The legend of this Peruvian skull is that it originated from Sirius and has an Atlantean vibe. Her shaman keeper uses it for healing. Nina's vibratory rate corresponds to the sixth dimension. When you apply your hands to Nina, she turns pink. She works for physical healing but also for longevity by acting on DNA and cells. Nina is used for people with physical and psychological problems.

"Establish contact with me so that I can bring the correct vibrational frequency back to your cells."

Her guardian: Irma

Date of discovery unknown

Material: Green beryl
Chakra: 4

Influences emotions and feelings. Symbol of calm and purity, it brings comfort and courage. Refreshes the etheric body and connects to the higher planes. Promotes prophetic dreams.

Weight: 8 lbs. / 3.5 kg

This beryl skull is the blue-green color of the sea. It has been passed from tribe to tribe, from Peru to Ecuador, Colombia, and finally Brazil. There it belonged to an Indian from a simple village in the Amazon rainforest. He gave it to Joky in 1997.

"Place me on your heart; let my message reach you."

His guardian: Joky Van Dieten

Discovered in Tiahuanaco, Bolivia (in the pre-Inca tradition)

Material: Rock crystal/quartz from Peru
Chakras: All 7 chakras

Universal healing stone for receiving, emitting, and amplifying. Unlocks blocked energies, transmits energy to the body, realigns subtle bodies.
    A stone that allows the awakening of consciousness, it helps develop concentration, intuition, telepathy, visualization, clairvoyance, and wisdom.

Weight: 12.5 lbs. / 5.7 kg

This skull has participated in many important ceremonies around the world, and since 2011 with Imanna. The three sacred animals of the Incas appear on the skull: the jaguar invites us into the secret power of the underworld, the serpent allows us to raise our energy like the Kundalini, and the condor opens the doors of heaven to us. Pacha Puma Huaca is the link between the heart of heaven and the heart of Earth /Mother. It allows you to be centered, to feel harmony and balance within yourself, and to find your luminous alignment to become the bridge between the worlds.

"Feel the life force flowing through you, nourished by the Pachamama you are, blessed by the Great Spirit you are."

Her guardian: Imanna
Website: www.imanna-crystalteam.com

Discovered in 1878

Material: Rock crystal or quartz
Chakras: All 7 chakras

Universal healing stone for receiving, emitting, and amplifying. Unlocks blocked energies, transmits energy to the body, realigns subtle bodies.

A stone that allows the awakening of consciousness, it helps develop concentration, intuition, telepathy, visualization, clairvoyance, and wisdom.

Weight: 5.5 lbs. / 2.54 kg

This skull was one of the first objects to enter the collections of the Ethnographic Museum of the Trocadéro in Paris, France, in 1878 (precursor of the Quai Branly Museum). It was donated to the museum by explorer Alphonse Pinart.

"As day follows night, all end is a beginning; all death is rebirth."

Its guardian: Quai Branly Museum
Website: www.quaibranly.fr

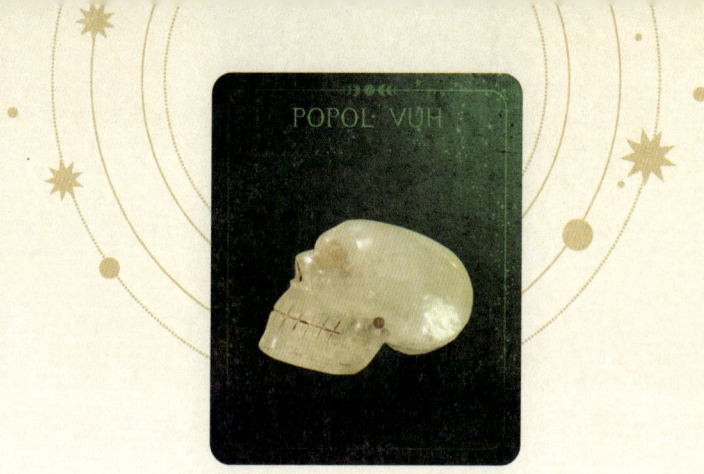

Discovered in Central America

Material: Rock crystal or quartz
Chakras: All 4 chakras

Universal healing stone for receiving, emitting, and amplifying. Unlocks blocked energies, transmits energy to the body, realigns subtle bodies.

A stone that allows the awakening of consciousness, it helps develop concentration, intuition, telepathy, visualization, clairvoyance, and wisdom.

Weight: Unknown

This long skull was part of a private collection of Mayan art donated by Jorge Castillo to the Popol Vuh Museum, on the campus of Francisco Marroquín University in Guatemala, in 1977. It is not known how he obtained it.

"I am the one who keeps and protects the energies of my clan, my tribe, my family here in Guatemala, on Earth and beyond the stars."

Its guardian: Popol Vuh Museum, Guatemala,
Mpv registration number 1543.

Website: https://popolvuh.ufm.edu

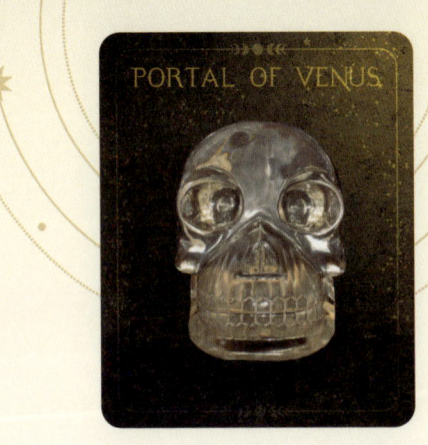

Date of discovery unknown

Material: Rock crystal or quartz
Chakras: All 7 chakras

Universal healing stone for receiving, emitting, and amplifying. Unlocks blocked energies, transmits energy to the body, realigns subtle bodies.
A stone that allows the awakening of consciousness, it helps develop concentration, intuition, telepathy, visualization, clairvoyance, and wisdom.

Weight: 14.9 lbs. / 6.80 kg

This skull is probably from China.

"I bring brilliance and clarity of mind and heart. I am helping you align with Unconditional Love. Connected to Sanat Kumara and Lady Venus, I remind you of our common and ancient bond with the planet Venus and the descent of Sanat Kumara, with the 144,000 light carriers to save our planet. It is to this high vibration of Unconditional Love that we return to this time of Earth/Mother Ascension."

His guardian: Alison James
Website: https://goldenageoflight.com

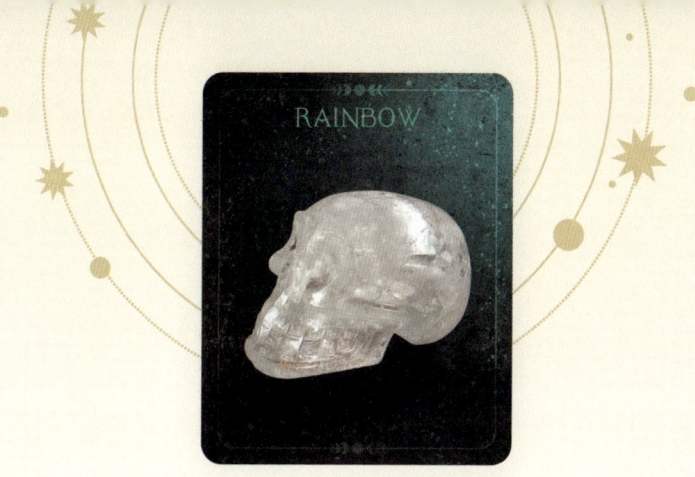

RAINBOW

Discovered in 1987

Material: Rock crystal or quartz
Chakras: All 4 chakras

Universal healing stone for receiving, emitting, and amplifying. Unlocks blocked energies, transmits energy to the body, realigns subtle bodies.

A stone that allows the awakening of consciousness, it helps develop concentration, intuition, telepathy, visualization, clairvoyance, and wisdom.

Weight: 6 lbs. / 2.8 kg

This skull has been the property of a Latin American family for more than 50 years and was inherited from the grandson of the owner, who says he received it from two priests in Guatemala.

"I am the path of light and color. I am the gateway to unlimited power. Open your mind and emotions to the powerful rays of light, to their full spectra. I am the path that leads to the magic of your mind."

His guardian: DaEl Walker
Website: https://crystalawareness.com

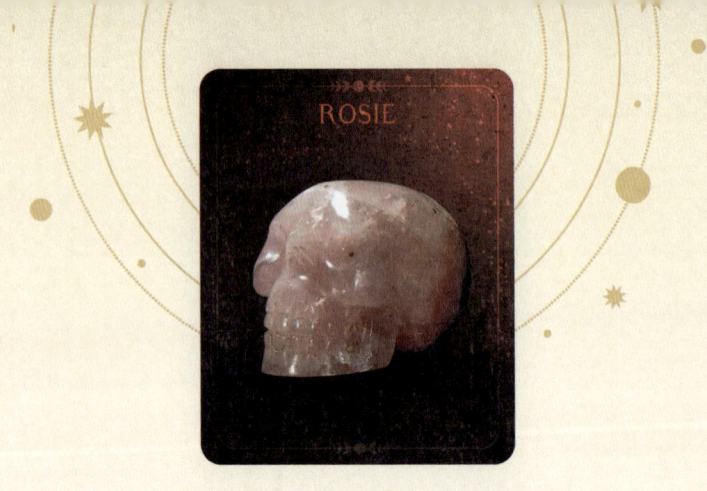

Discovered in 1994

Material: Rose quartz
Chakra: 4

Stone of peace and unconditional love. Purifies and opens the heart, releases negative emotions, increases discernment and self-love. Strengthens empathy and the ability to love.

Weight: 13.2 lbs. / 6 kg

It was discovered in the state of Puebla, Mexico, during the opening of a new road. The skull rolled down the hill. I believe this is the only rose quartz skull discovered that has been described as genuine.

"Peace. Receive lots of Love, positive healing energy."

His guardian: Jaime Maussan
Website: www.tercermilenio.tv

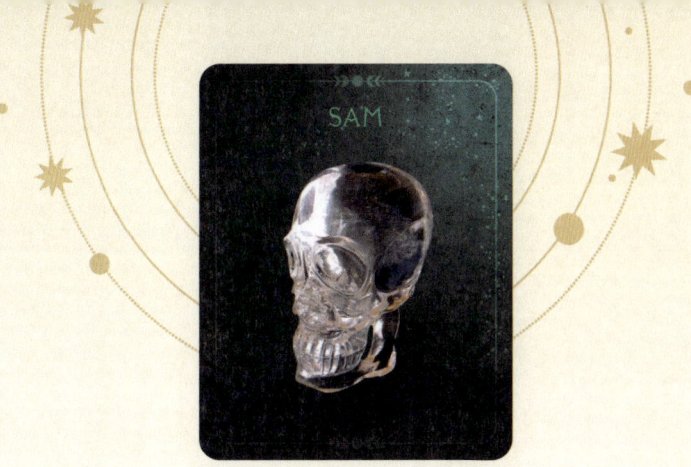

Date of discovery unknown

Material: Rock crystal or quartz
Chakras: All 4 chakras

Universal healing stone for receiving, emitting, and amplifying. Unlocks blocked energies, transmits energy to the body, realigns subtle bodies.

A stone that allows the awakening of consciousness, it helps develop concentration, intuition, telepathy, visualization, clairvoyance, and wisdom.

Weight: 12 lbs. / 5.44 kg

It seems that this skull was carved in Brazil by an unknown sculptor who carved only a single skull. Whatever the truth, Sam's style is unique and quirky.

"I invite you to be more aware. Become who you really are by expanding your awareness and by transforming your belief structures, replacing them with knowledge and understanding. As you open up to the energies of the crystal in general, and mine in particular, you will be guided to tap into the vast fields of knowledge available, both on Earth and in the infinite realms of the universe."

His guardian: Jaap Van Etten
Website: www.lemurantis.com

Discovered in 1995

Material: Rock crystal or quartz
Chakras: All 7 chakras

Universal healing stone for receiving, emitting, and amplifying. Unlocks blocked energies, transmits energy to the body, realigns subtle bodies.

A stone that allows the awakening of consciousness, it helps develop concentration, intuition, telepathy, visualization, clairvoyance, and wisdom.

Weight: 13.2 lbs. / 5.98 kg

Authentic, this ancient crystal skull was discovered in Guerrero, Mexico, by F.R . Nick Nocerino using psychic archeology.

"My message is unconditional acceptance. Just as there are many trails leading to the top of the mountain, each individual has a unique way of walking their path. As a shamanic tool, I illuminate the path of the individual linked to that of all of humanity."

His guardian: Michele Nocerino
Website: https://crystalskulls.com/michele-nocerino.html

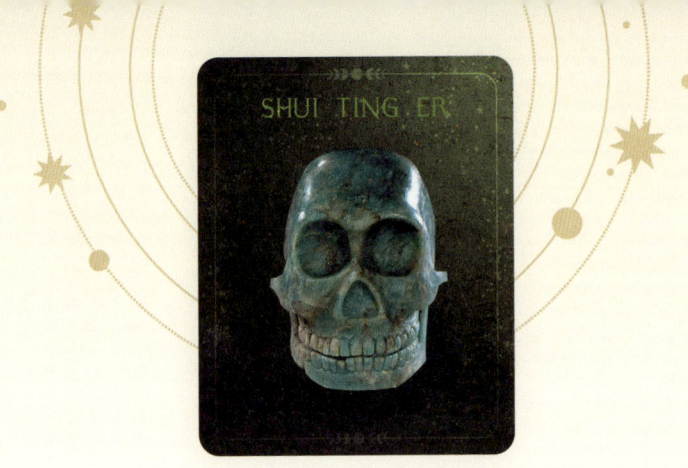

Discovered in 1860

Material: Amazonite
Chakras: 4 and 5

Its effect is soothing. Excellent stone against depression. Unlocks physical, emotional, and mental blockages. Promotes concentration and independence. Helps unite intuition and reality.

Weight: 11.2 lbs. / 5.1 kg

This skull is native to southwestern Mongolia, near the Chinese border. It was discovered over 160 years ago by a Chinese archeologist named Yeng Fo Huu. In the 1930s, a Danish missionary, Pastor Utkielen, was able to purchase this unique skull from the archeologist's family. Pastor Utkielen's family donated the skull to Joky in 1992.

"Place me on your heart; let my message reach you."

His guardian: Joky Van Dieten

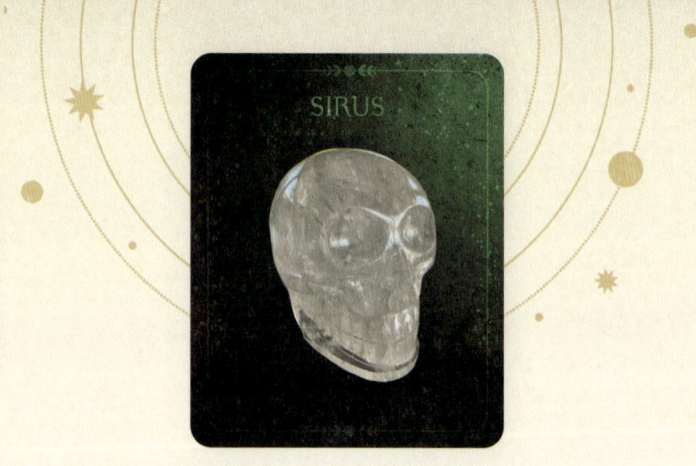

Sculpted in 2004 in Brazil

Material: Rock crystal or quartz
Chakras: All 7 chakras

Universal healing stone for receiving, emitting, and amplifying. Unlocks blocked energies, transmits energy to the body, realigns subtle bodies.
A stone that allows the awakening of consciousness, it helps develop concentration, intuition, telepathy, visualization, clairvoyance, and wisdom.

Weight: 17.8 lbs. / 8.1 kg

Loaded with ancient knowledge, in contact with other ancient skulls (such as the Mitchell-Hedges skull, Max, and Sha Na Ra), and used in ceremonies and on sacred sites (such as those in Mexico, Guatemala, Peru, Stonehenge, Easter Island, and Crop Circles), he has a special connection with the dolphins and the energies of Sirius—the planet known as the home of the gods, the heavenly paradise. The Egyptians associated him with the goddess Isis. From there our ancestors would have come to populate the earth.

"I facilitate the 'Earth Sky' connection, which allows us to connect with our place of origin and Earth/Mother. Listen to the teaching of our guides about dolphins that open the heart chakra."

His guardian: Patrice Marty
Website: www.moncranedecristal.fr

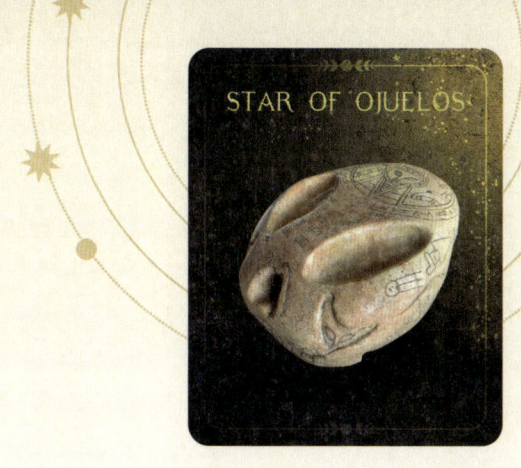

STAR OF OJUELOS

Discovered in 2018 and dated to approximately 6000 to 1800 BCE

Material: Unknown

Weight: 11 lbs. / 4.9 kg

It was discovered in Cerro del Toro, Ojuelos de Jalisco, Mexico. I acquired it in 2019 during an international congress where I was invited to give a lecture on the Mysterious Stones. Known for decades or more by their inhabitants, these stones have often been passed down from generation to generation in the form of family and heritage collections. It is believed that Aztlan beings lived here in the mythical land of the Aztecs.

"I am a twinkling star in the Milky Way and in your heart; lovingly connect with this part of the star."

His guardian: Patrice Marty
Website: www.moncranedecristal.fr

Discovered before 1945

Material: Gold
Chakra: 7

Symbolizes the nobility of heart. Illuminates the mind and promotes connection with our being of light. Intensifies positive feelings. Gives meaning to life and encourages actions of great value.

Weight: 1.3 lbs. / 600 g

The exact date of its discovery is unknown, but it was likely after World War II.

"May the light of the Sun of Tibet shine on the world where peace, love, and harmony prevail."

His guardian: Dr. Frank Loo

SYNERGY

Discovered in 1981

Material: Rock crystal or quartz
Chakras: All 7 chakras

Universal healing stone for receiving, emitting, and amplifying. Unlocks
blocked energies, transmits energy to the body, realigns subtle bodies.
    A stone that allows the awakening of consciousness, it helps develop
concentration, intuition, telepathy, visualization, clairvoyance, and wisdom.

Weight: 15.4 lbs. / 7 kg

The skull was the property of a nun who had received it from a shaman from
the Pacific. Then, this skull was acquired in a village in the Andes by a
businessman. An elder native told him that the skull had chosen him. Finally,
the skull met its current owner, Sherry, in 2001 in the United States.

"The first thing to do with a skull is to 'remember.' In reality,
you are a being of light. You are a spiritual being within a physical body.
Remember. . ."

His guardian: Sherry Whitfield
Website: www.crystal-skulls.com

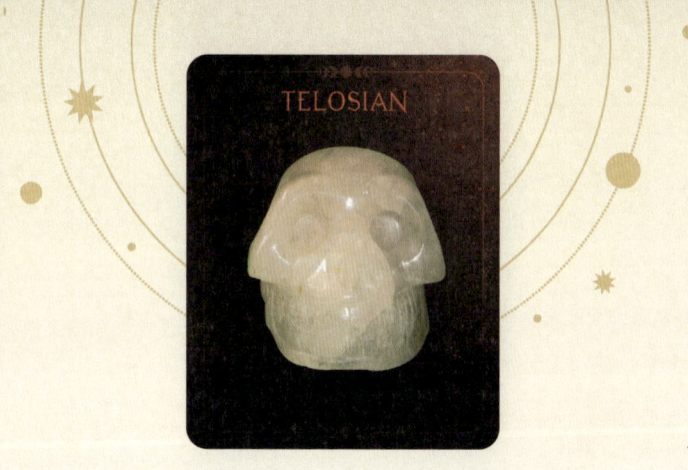

Date of discovery unknown

Material: Rock crystal or quartz
Chakras: All 7 chakras

Universal healing stone for receiving, emitting, and amplifying. Unlocks blocked energies, transmits energy to the body, realigns subtle bodies.

A stone that allows the awakening of consciousness, it helps develop concentration, intuition, telepathy, visualization, clairvoyance, and wisdom.

Weight: 15.4 lbs. / 7 kg

Unknown story.

"This skull has a deep and powerful resonance with Telos and the ancient Lemurian energies, as well as with the beings below Mount Shasta. The Telosians await the acceleration of humanity into the fifth dimensional energies of Divine Love. Master Adama, the high priest of Telos, is ready to aid those who rise to Unconditional Love through the Telosian skull."

His guardian: Alison James
Website: https://goldenageoflight.com

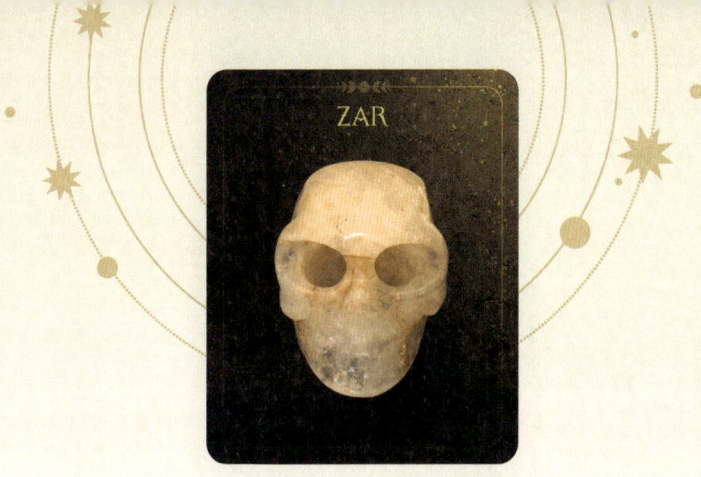

Discovered in 1995

Material: Rock crystal or quartz
Chakras: All 7 chakras

Universal healing stone for receiving, emitting, and amplifying. Unlocks blocked energies, transmits energy to the body, realigns subtle bodies.

A stone that allows the awakening of consciousness, it helps develop concentration, intuition, telepathy, visualization, clairvoyance, and wisdom.

Weight: 9.7 lbs. / 4.4 kg.

Zar comes from the Pleiades. It would have been carved from alien quartz. He came here four million years ago, as a gift from a mysterious group. Zar's personality is calm, very wise, and unpretentious. Zar is a specialist in the spectrum of human emotions. He can help you stabilize other people's emotions. Zar loves flowers.

"I am here to help you understand yourself, stabilize yourself, and control the greatest power you have: your emotions. Reactivate your spiritual path through meditation with me and recover your divine essence."

His guardian: DaEl Walker
Website: https://crystalawareness.com

About the AUTHOR

PATRICE MARTY,
researcher of the inexplicable

For most people, trying to find explanations for the mysteries of life is a waste of time; for Patrice Marty, it is a must! And for him, it started at a young age.

Attracted by skulls since his childhood, Patrice drew them everywhere: in his notebooks, school books, journals. . . and they are still a source of inspiration for him today.

Patrice's interest was piqued in his teens, when, in a book, he discovered the crystal skull of explorer F. Mitchell-Hedges. Skulls would no longer be just a childhood interest to him. . . they would become his quest!

At this point, Patrice began to research different civilizations and cultures and their relationships to skulls, as well as the history of these crystal artifacts that straddle the line between myth and reality. Patrice reconnected to the energy of the crystal skulls during his first contact with Max, one of the ancient skulls of Mayan legend, in 2003 in The Netherlands: this fateful meeting would change the course of his life!

Patrice then understood why he had always been drawn to crystal skulls. He knew that he was destined to become one of the carriers of their history.

Today, as the guardian of several skulls (both modern and old), Patrice gives lectures and travels the world.

In search of discovering new skulls and on the trail of ancient civilizations, he organizes trips to share his passion and his experience, including Mexico (where in 2005 he received his Mayan baptism by Kayum, his brother from the Lacandón tribe of Palenque), Guatemala, Peru, Bolivia, Easter Island, Bosnia, and England (Stonehenge, Glastonbury, and various Crop Circles).

Patrice is the former organizer of the Festival of Crystal Skulls in France, where he hosted major ancient skulls and many shamans.

Today he organizes wellness and therapy fairs all over France and online at www.salonsbienetre.com.

Discover the skulls and more information on Patrice's
various journeys by visiting his website at www.savoirperdu.com
or www.moncranedecristal.fr.

Encounter between the Sirius skull and a dolphin

Design by Brenda McCallum
Type set in Narnia/BentonSans/Minion Pro

Translation Consultant: Séverine Jeauneau
Images and text for the skulls provided by the guardians.

Copyrights for selected photos and texts: Paris Skull (p. 64): © 2010, Musée du quai Branly (photo Patrick Gries / Valérie Torre / Scala, Florence); British Museum Skull (p. 33): © Trustees of the British Museum; Popol Vuh (p. 65): © 2015, photo Patrice Marty; Chakras illustrations (p. 11): Oksana Pravdina—AdobeStock; Virgin of Guadalupe image (p. 18 [[?]]): AdobeStock; Copyrights for the French edition © 2020, Éditions Exergue, an imprint of Guy Trédaniel

ISBN: 978-0-7643-6534-8
Printed in China

Published by REDFeather Mind, Body, Spirit
An imprint of Schiffer Publishing, Ltd.
4880 Lower Valley Road
Atglen, PA 19310
Phone: (610) 593-1777; Fax: (610) 593-2002
Email: Info@redfeathermbs.com
Web: www.redfeathermbs.com

For our complete selection of fine books on this and related subjects, please visit our website at www.redfeathermbs.com. You may also write for a free catalog.